LOTUS BUFFET

Special thanks to Patricia Waters, Memye Curtis Tucker, Cecilia Woloch and Ginger Murchison for their encouragement and suggestions as these poems evolved. Thanks also to the Atlanta poetry community in all its incarnations, to everyone associated with The Farm and its ongoing vision and especially to Kathy for her support, patience and tough-love critiques.

Acknowledgements:

My thanks to the editors of the following publications where some of the poems in this book first appeared.

Origins of Hell – *Natural Bridge*

At the Art Brut Show – *Backwards City Review*

On the Approach of Jehovah's Witnesses – *Cumberland Poetry Review*

You Probably Had to Be There
Why Reading *Anna Karenina* Takes a Long Time – *FutureCycle*

Where Flesh Begins – *Borderlands, Texas Review of Poetry*

Toast – *Java Monkey Anthology, Vol III*

Jody Leaves the County – *Dark Sky Magazine*

Fourth and Fifth Periods, 1962 – *Snake Nation Review*

On the Stonehenge Bus – *Ouroborous Review*

Feedback
My Favorite Line from *Howard's End* – *Earthshine*

Aunt Weeza Sees a Condom on the Side of the Road,
The Morning After George Segal Died – *A Celebration of Southern Poets, Kennesaw State Press*

Faulkner, Jung and the 60 Cycle Hum – *storySouth*

To the December Birds While Re-Filling
Their Backyard Feeder – *The Cortland Review*

Care
Prideful Buddhist – *Blue Fifth Review*

Radical Rhetoric
My Grandfather's Ruined Cabin
First Commune Winter – *An Anthology of Southern Poetry,* Texas
      Review Press

Cover Photo

—University of Tennessee Medical School, 1912

My grandfather wrote, *Lab*, on the back
before sending it to his mother
whose own mother kept an 1840s diary,
whole days in up-country Carolina
with *Spun* as their one entry . . . or. . . *So lonely*.
But look where their boy is now—
limitless science, gas from the ceiling,
more flasks than you could shake a stick at,
microscopes, tubes and such windows—
what allowed the perfect light of a world
not at war to stream in, show us the way.

Contents

Draughts of the Warm South

Notes to Seymour's Fat Lady

"But I'll tell you a terrible secret—Are you listening to me? There isn't anyone out there who isn't Seymour's Fat Lady."

—J.D. Salinger, *Franny and Zooey*

My Favorite Line from *Howard's End*

You must alter yourself, or we shan't
have happy lives.

Oh, the surety of Edwardian wisdom.
Imperious as their beloved dead Queen,
these sisterly words (from wise to foolish)
still convey a heft: *We're in this together*,
basis of all girl-talk, what traces its way
back to some cave or, okay, just outside—
two squat females with honed slate
scraping flesh from a yet-warm hide
while multi-tasking, softly conspiring
for their greater good, swapping notes
regarding *his* temper, how to avoid it,
their only tools a coded eye-roll,
a whispered heads-up like the above,
Margaret's wish that Helen dump her project,
her protégée, the sad-sack cockney clerk,
Helen's urge to better him a burden,
a leaden yoke on their shared neck,
Margaret's words so the same as Krishna's
when Arjuna declared he would not fight,
swaths of the Gita devoted to this:
Warriors war . . . because that is their station.
Same as poor clerks must hold situations,
same as Forster must write and (if we believe
Naipaul) have his way with Bengali boys
before living on . . . even through the '60s,
the time-traveler outside whose window
a strange, empire-less England swung . . .
Mods, Rockers, Stones and Twiggys in full swirl,

Helen's rejection of class gone global—
all of us still lifting our eyes unto the hills,
but our help these days cometh from within.
We dream, we parade, we weep, we bugger.
We're still not quite there. We want happy lives.

Cleaning the Coffee Table, Saturday Night

There's a sadness to last Sunday's *Times*,
still unread, now heaped with junk mail.
In its youth each story held such promise,
prompting that caffeinated vow, *I'll get to it*—
the class of lie we feed ourselves daily.
But no, these sections will not be read.
In *Style* you're not going to recognize
the candid Hamptons shot of Joan LeBeau,
her post-wedding dazzler of a smile
a half-beat behind that same breezy hair—
Gemini Joan, still with her signature wattage,
the energy you circled, fed upon for years,
the news that Joan has married up
arriving not so much as a shock
than as confirmation of assumed grief.

But you never saw her picture, did you?
No, you cleared the table, buried the paper,
covered all with layers of cans and wine bottles
before dragging the recycle bin to the curb
where, come Monday, Andres of the heavy gloves
will dump Joan's now Chianti-stained smile
for it's all pulp to him, all dead weight.
And when Andres bends low for the quick snatch,
the agony of a right-eye-socket hangover
will rebound with that cruel post-tequila throb . . .
what demands the ancient question:
How will I make it through this day?

Feedback

As arguments at Shane's Hideaway go,
this one was civil, the after-work crowd
debating which guitarist had first formed
an actual note from feedback, raw sound—
who had done it, tamed what's infinite,
the Jeff Beck champions up by the taps
taking on two Dick Dale dudes by the limes,
until barmaid Missy from Sussex,
she of the half-shaved head and tongue stud,
declared us all *proper wankers* for not knowing
it was George Harrison, his lead-in buzz-whine
to *I Feel Fine* (an F#, she said) in 1965.

We were all pretty much afraid of Missy
so we pointed for another round
and kept it to ourselves that, wait, no,
it must have been Les Paul who more or less
invented the electric guitar.
Surely Les, early on, down in his basement,
was twisting knobs, messing around as usual,
the volume a bit cranked, the amp too close,
and here it came, Pluto's underworld wail,
sine waves chasing their electron tails,
Les taking two quick steps back—there!
a sonic G, unmistakably a note,
all while Fermi pulled graphite rods from a core,
while Pollock dripped in two dimensions
this new world in a grain of sand, silicone,
what could be baked, sliced so thin, charged . . .
Les unaware, smiling at what he'd wrought,
Mary Ford yelling down the stairs again,
"Honey, please! You know that scares the cats."

To the December Birds While
Re-Filling Their Feeder

You can come back now . . . okay?
And look, it's that oily sunflower seed,
the boutique stuff you pecked all April . . .
back when your plumage was, well,
let's not get into it at that level
though it would be truthful to admit
how your current dull gray-browns
never make me reach for the camera
because, like Hardy's solitary thrush
singing non-stop out on Dorset's bare limbs,
you're darkling for a Darwinian cause—
sexual hues are unneeded till spring.

But now it is winter. My feet are cold.
And in the spirit of full disclosure
I'll admit to balking at the seed's cost
when, in a store, I recalled your feeder,
rank stinginess disguised as moral qualms
over one species feeding another.
Too late though, we're already symbiotic,
hopelessly so—there's no going back same as
the pigeon-feeding woman downtown,
who, with bread-crumb bestowing arms,
assumes the pure stance of St Francis
when clearly she's not him—she's over-layered,
soup-kitchened, beat down but for moments
when she tracks the low afternoon sun,
when, with eyes closed, she inhabits grace,
what's there for each of us, only waiting.

Longshoremen, 1969

Ding-dinging cable cars growled beneath
the windows of our cat-stink Polk Street flat,
windows we kept open to hear fog horns,
to breathe the fog itself for we were
just-arrived hip-enfants from the South
dumb enough to rent rooms where hookers
      turned loud tricks next door,
 where sallow-cheeked junkies
      tied-off down a dark hallway.
Yet we united into family,
we looked out for each other,
but mostly they looked out for us:
   You're acid heads! You can get on welfare!
      The word, *welfare*, meaning ATD,
      beloved letters of the street and park—
      Aid to the Totally Disabled—
California's compassion offered
to the waves of spiritually confused,
yes, disabled, showing up every day.
But we ignored the lumpen's advice,
judging it wrong to accept State alms,
adhering instead to the beatnik model,
      seekers who fancied themselves sadhus—
      which we certainly weren't. Were! Weren't.
No matter, we made stabs at Buddha's
      suggestions, the eight-fold-path,
Right Livelihood by far the hardest,
Right Livelihood propelling us
      out the morning door,
      down to the docks,
      to ILWU Number Two
where anyone could get a union card,

where we waited for our numbers,
hollered from a steel meshed window.
        The stewards had guns.
        Lena's, a soul food dive next door,
served the blackest coffee, the hottest grits,
and on the juke box poor dead Otis
        kept on singing his song,
        kept on singing our song—
        how he left his home in Georgia,
        how he headed to this bay . . .
where great ships called so we could descend,
clean their rusty holds, scraping
then mucking out heavy mud sludge,
the filth of the world accumulated.
        And there, content we could go no lower,
we bent to our calling, emptying hulls,
lifting freighters higher in the water,
        raising ships, this was it—*Right Livelihood!*
We were still confused of course but useful.
It was Charles Manson summer down in LA,
        and here, out in the bay, Indians
        had captured Alcatraz where they painted
        slogans on sheets hung from cellblock windows.
Cassady had been found cold, dead in Mexico.
Ginsberg was off to Europe, Snyder in Japan,
        the Beats gone, all gone.
We'd missed the party but didn't know it,
so we did what we thought we should do—
        we sat till it hurt at the Zen Center,
        danced with Sufi Sam,
        smoked chillums with fakirs,
        ate sugary butter balls with Krishnas,
        threw sapphron coins while
faking comprehension of the I Ch'ing,

although *Perseverance furthers* was quite clear.
We ate peyote then lay on the floor
    vibrating while the hookers and junkies
    let themselves in and laughed,
making sport of us, yelling once more,
    Get on ATD!!
    (two beat pause) *Stupid hicks . . .*
But no. Mornings found us on the 30 Stockton
down to the docks, to the union, to Lena's,
    to Pier 47 or maybe Oakland
    where again we ended up
below the water line
    yet somehow afloat.
    Knees stiff from Right Practice,
we shoveled black gunk, trying not to gag
before whistling for the big hook
to drop below-decks, to jerk our sludge bin
    straight up,
    where we had to look,
    where we had to follow its progress,
take in the one sky, the world's cover,
that small piece of it we were allotted
from the bottom hold of a freighter—
    it was a square of deep blue,
    and sometimes, if we were lucky,
    we'd see a gull.

Anniversary Dinner at a Trendy Little Place

Bad enough we have to valet the pick-up,
but when the server attends us with a crumb brush
I lean back too far, a child in the way
wary of Daddy's, *Let a man do his job!*
Not that the old man had a job himself,
he remained drunk, his tools pretty much bound
by rust to the metal box, to each other
from the ongoing porch leak, but so what,
this was just how files and wrenches looked,
coated in a fine red, almost Martian dust.
The leak too was quite normal, overhead
boards in full sag, chocolate cake rot,
the one uncle who would spread tar up there
died early, before dharma transmission.
And so the lessening continued, the slide—
I handed out Donkey Kong quarters
to my girls instead of walking Dickens dolls
across coffee tables the way great aunts
had done for me while speaking Pip's lines.

But this is now—the aunts are long dead
and the daughters time-zones away,
leaving us to enjoy our river dinner
where we eat too much crusty bread,
even asking for more like field hands,
Ma and Pa Kettle gone to a brasserie.
We make crumbs in service to entropy,
the Shakers' fate present, hovering—
we drop the ball, forget verse, lose rings,
centers can't hold, and fled is that music
from us all on this long downhill skid
under a sun they all say will one day implode.

Why Reading *Anna Karenina*
Takes a Long Time

> *. . . The discussion concerned the fashionable question of*
> *whether there was a dividing line between the mental and*
> *physiological phenomena in human activity, and if so,*
> *where?*
>
> —page 51, Signet, Magarshack
> translation

What first stops us is the word, *fashionable,*
how laughable it sounds in this parlor
Tolstoy imagines—of the landed gentry,
those who continue to work peasants while
tossing French idioms, affecting Parisian airs
when all of France thought Russia feudal, brutal.

But the question, let's not duck the question
because it's still a bit of an intrigue, no?
And since brain capillaries would be the place
to start, we borrow that microscopic submarine
from Fantastic Voyage, complete with Raquel Welch.
But into whose head? Anna's? A peasant's? The Count's?

Wait, let's go for Freud's, his source of thought,
our craft forging upstream, to the end of all blood,
and there, aground in Synaptic Swamp,
coughing, fanning pipe smoke residue
we abandon ship and press on to Nameless Mesa
where we're dazzled by ozone vistas, ions,

free electrons streaking through on missions,
And vus zat leetle boy yew? drifts by,
fueled by strudel, cocaine, Viennese cognac.
Raquel runs after *What do women want?*
and becomes lost beneath boiling skies.
We don't like it here. We missed a turn.

On the Stonehenge Bus

It's October so there's plenty of room
as we board outside Salisbury's rail station
where Hardy allowed Jude (the Obscure)
to shiver in its "fireless" rooms with Sue,
his cousin, repressed love, his millstone.
Today though, another couple's in crisis,
German backpackers who halt at the door
of our logo-ed, speaker-filled transport
and ask for, "Zee lo-cal . . . vid no tour-ests,"
what produces instant camaraderie
among us, the seated, as the driver laughs,
explains that the local will take them
only to Old Sarum where they would still face
a four-mile walk plus the site admission
included in the ticket we have bought,
we the easy-way-takers, a spread out
comfy unit of Euro-Asian-Yanks
unwilling to even consider hiking half the day
across a windy plain to what surely
would be more appreciated, more cathartic
were it to be first sighted from stone-tired legs,
a trade-off the couple now appears to debate
with the passion reserved for moral choices.
And as the door closes, as the tape loop starts,
Our journey begins in the medieval city . . .
this is when they're rapping for entry,
paying, moving with heads down to the back
as though to meet any of our eyes would be
a taint, an admission of compromise—

and there on the long row they sit, beat down,
as far apart as possible, each with a window,
yet neither bothering to look as we near
the impossibly tall cathedral where Jude,
denied Oxford by love, instead chipped stone.

Radical Rhetoric

We lived in college-rental shanties
across the tracks from a hosiery mill
where actual *workers* (the word we so loved)
showed up every day in their ailing cars.
They, of course, lived in far-better houses
than our listing shacks so it would have been
the bohemian poor trying to instruct
a lower-middle-class who hated us.
Still we adhered to the notion because
it cast us in the soft light of *struggle*,
a romantic fable starring ourselves.

We were snobs, and we used drugs, bad ones,
bashing inhalers with bricks in the driveway,
deranged cavemen intent on a new treat,
the amphetamine soaked cotton wick
(what also contained a potent menthol),
our short-cut to the wisdom of ages,
fully understandable for twelve hours,
blessed window to cram then pass finals
that, if failed, started the slide to Viet Nam.
Our study nights began with discipline
before the arrival of great insights
never once remembered the next day,
breakthrough visions stopped for nose-holding
mentholated burps that repelled modish
art school girls who might have briefly thought us
intriguing when we sang, "Che! Che! Che!"
to Aretha's song, when we partied
at the pace of the hated frat boys who'd
soon be exploiting the poor *workers,*
the *proles* we would save at some future date,

those faithful who answered the mill's whistle
twice daily, what sometimes made us fist-pump,
yell, "Quitting Time!" in *solidarity*,
when outside, if we had bothered to look,
their cars had just pulled in, doors were slamming.
It was early on a frosty morning,
and a new diamond dew covered the world.

At the Art Brut Show

*Eva Droppova's paintings are inspired by questions addressed
to the Spirit World and take shape in language understood
only by the artist . . .*
    —Curator's notes

Well, isn't that always the way?
Especially with difficult work,
what sits on the wall or the page
or what offends a preconceived ear
can be an icy slope with no Sherpas
where it's up to you to ax out footholds,
supposing all the way this, no, maybe that
tack will lead to a least a base camp
(what's illusory anyway) of *understanding,*
where we kid ourselves, though it is a rush,
that we've divined artistic lingua.

It likely began in Mrs. Nash's Second Grade
with glances over to Jennifer's drawing
because your manila resisted any first,
irretrievable mark, even a child's horizon,
the line that can never be wrong.
Yet Jennifer across the table was in the zone,
in dialogue with those 16 Crayola Gods,
humming at the same time even,
her nail-bitten fingers autonomic.

But God forbid she ends up like Eva Droppova,
round-the-bend from a son's suffering,
locked up tightly in her Bratislava house
yet with access to felt-tip pens, paper,
and where, apparently, someone visited,
someone who contacted a gallery friend,

and now the world approaches her work.
Or is this but rank appropriation,
to listen in on Eva Droppova's
conversations with the Spirit World.
It's almost like those stories from great-aunts
of the old party-lines, when phone calls
sometimes crossed, when it must have taken
an overwhelming push of propriety to not listen
as strange voices played out strange lives,
to instead softly put the receiver down.
But a painting or a play or a carved
piece of soap is different, isn't it?
Different at least from eavesdropping
on Eva Droppova's transforming pain.
That is, the play or soap or etching
aspires to be an intercepted message.
We want others to notice us as we
petition the Spirit World in public
on purpose with perhaps the hope of money.

Oftentimes though, there's an iron-poor
operator on duty at Spirit World central,
her switchboard headset at a rakish angle.
She reminds us of Lily Tomlin's Ernestine
popping gum and snorting while
daydreaming of what, menfriend? Her own art?
All the time pushing home connections
to (hopefully) the few world souls
equipped to listen, able to pull soul
from what's deep code-talk to the rest of us
stranded out here on our normal island.

Levitation Gone Wrong

Gas! Gas! Quick, boys! An ecstasy of fumbling . . .
—Wilfred Owen, *Dulce et Decorum Est*

It turns out we'd been tear-gassed together
    at the Levitation of the Pentagon, 1967,
and as the visiting Great Man stands
    surrounded by a punch bowl circle,
I can't stop myself from pushing our bond:
    "The Potomac really stunk, didn't it?"
He shrugs, gives the slightest sigh.
    "We were like this parade of Santas," I go on,
"Chanting, 'Ho, Ho, Ho . . . Chi Minh.'"
    Nobody laughs . . . because he doesn't,
and I get the message to just . . . shut . . . up.
    "Hippie chicks," he eventually allows,
his smile savoring some lost promise.
    "They were the only reason I was there."
Now comes laughter at this witticism,
    a certified *bon mot* from the quotable,
what combines a rebuke to the suck-up
    with fair notice that his potency lives.
He turns to a smiling woman in silk
    who, even forewarned, leans from the waist.

The autumn afternoon went from warm dusk
    to cool dark so quickly it was as though
the planet had conspired to spin faster.
    Shells landed behind us, soft, on target
canisters trailing plumes of pale yellow
    (the Great Man at least agrees on that).
Ranks of the 82nd Airborne boys laughed
    from behind tight green masks at us,

so unequipped, the Armies of the Night
    brought low, in full retreat now, crying,
stripping t-shirts to serve as half-ass veils.
    An ecstasy of fumbling? Perhaps,
but our coughs were trivial next to Owen's.
    We coughed nonetheless, speed-crawling
across endless Pentagon parking lots,
    porch dogs with no business on a hunt,
gasping on curbed islands of grass
    as routed Yippies ran past screaming,
People this and *Revolution* that . . . all in mere
    tear gas, distant cousin to mustard gas,
the Great War's scourge—what burnt lungs,
    blistered exposed skin, blinded, what sank
a generation of hollow-eyed young men
    onto park benches all across England.

Owen, Siegfried Sassoon and Robert Graves
    convalesced near Edinburgh in 1918,
Graves shell-shocked and so sexually confused
    yet loyal still to the lost cause of slaughter
in the name of Victoria's demented kin.
    Sassoon even drafted a letter to Parliament
decrying the "Scarlet Majors," but Graves, sensing
    the hand of Bertrand Russell, repressed it,
all while Owen wrote *Anthem for Doomed Youth*
    in those summer months at Craiglockhart,
a brownstone fortress of a hospital, the building
    still there but now with double-paned windows,
a trendy, retro landmark for an urban college,
    last stop on the 23 line of Lothian transport
whose drivers "deserve the right to work
    without fear of assault," the route winding

first down from the Royal Mile before
    traversing the neighborhoods where both
Harry Potter and *Grand Theft Auto* were born
    before up, up to Craiglockhart's hill perch,
the hill Owen left later that summer when he returned
    to his unit, his duty, the Front, his death
with the Artists' Fuseliers only days before Armistice,
    the hill from which Edinburgh Castle
and even the Firth are visible, a horizon world,
    a cardboard cut-out of a place somehow at peace,
the same view they must have so enjoyed
    when winds swept the choking coal dust to sea.

Care

As my mother's mouth lesions worsened,
making a jail-break from gums to face,
I entered the old house twice daily
to puree the Stouffer's Turkey Noodle Alfredo,
a whitish goo that somehow sustained life,
her bedroom Sony blaring even louder
as though the blender's whine were a threat
to the love between TV and dying woman.
And after her thanks for food and water
I often searched for some unneeded lie
to escape this air where part of my mother
was out-gassing, returning to dirt
before the rest of her was ready to go,
what had made the surgeon lean to her ear,
     There's nothing more we can do for you, Sara,
what at least fetched the home hospice corps—
habitless holy women who brought
the vigor of a new sheriff in town, plus new drugs.
They said everything I was doing was right.
They said taking care of the care-giver
carried equal weight, and this I believed
for this was their calling, to be escorts,
transition-queens whose word was made law.
So, really, how wrong could it have been
to sometimes late at night unscrew the sticky top
from the Roxanol, synthetic morphine,
so thick, so cherry-flavored, so mythic.
And there on the front porch where, as a boy
I licked red popsicles before they melted,
I now saw tail lights smear to ruby streaks.
We both took the kiss of all Gods rising.

Jack's Royal Comes In

Here's why we sift through volumes of letters:
in response to Ginsberg's rambling notes
(fun in Sodom just the latest) all Kerouac
can offer from a pre-Disney Orlando
(where he's taking care of his mother)
is that his typewriter's now at some shop
for a twenty-seven buck overhaul
where whoever was assigned the machine
must have given a slow whistle—
Jesus. Check out this Royal!

Shredded ribbon, stuck *Shift* key, bent strikers
all pointing to the non-stop pounding
this baby had taken while being force-fed
not single sheets of paper but eternal
scrolls scotch-taped together ascending
snakelike from dusty floors, charmed by the bell's
all-night *dings* at each line's skidding end,
a cry for help before the beat carriage
took the slap-slam back left for more
Benzedrine-fueled punishment,
so the poor letters again could get smacked
from their choir-loft positions to strike
the tired ribbon a good one, *o's* and *p's*
going cloudy within days, each entry
a violence, a jab or hook scoring solid
imprinting hits, *animal v machine*,
what would later prompt Truman Capote's
famous bitch to David Suskind,
"That isn't writing. It's type-writing."

This was the baggage dropped on their shop—
the heraldic, Hellenic typewriter
soon to launch thousands of VW buses,
the link of austere East to be-bop West.
But the green-visored guys cared not
for Mahayana concerns. They were pros
who first triaged then hunched over it
for at least a day, given the tab,
and a week later Kerouac was writing,
"This is the smoothest typewriter ever!
Even if the ribbon still feeds only one way,
and they forgot to return the legs."

Easy, Jack—just think of our poor boys,
stuck under bad shop lights in that yellow
cigaretted and coffeed '50s air
while outside, off-shore breezes were blowing
distractions from both coasts.
PCB-less fish were biting, jumping.
Plus other, normal, typewriters waited
on the table where Kim from Bookkeeping
(so stacked!) sometimes paused to lean, laugh,
agree to non-specific promises
for that after-work drink. All were sleepy
from staying up to watch Jack Paar,
their dicks restless from the promise of Kim,
the more they looked, the more they found
wounded on this beater from the scruffy guy
who surely did not expect much of a bill,
so, as on all jobs in all times

a stopping point had to be found, enforced.
Someone declared the Royal "good enough."
And even though they knew a stern uncle
would have said they could have done more,
they went ahead and yellow-tagged the thing.
They pushed it aside. They wrote out the ticket.

Late Renaissance BO in
the Permanent Collection

Forget the on-loan show from the Louvre
two floors above. Here we find solitude,
no guards near this four-foot square canvas
used by an unknown Venetian to depict
the rape scene from II Samuel where
Amnon, bad-boy son of David, assaults
Tamar, no matter she has just brought
special treats, the plates now scattered,
her bodice yanked well south of breasts,
the soft girl turning with a defensive arm
in what appears less the refusal
of a half-brother's unwanted advances
than a reflex move to avoid his armpit,
torso, the harsh wind of abscessed teeth.

The model for Amnon was put-together,
ripped, we might say today, complete
with a gym-less six pack, each ab
definition enhanced by the brooding
Italianate light, each pore shiny,
out-gassing what it must—essence of *him,*
rank canal urchin perhaps, now grown,
enticed here by money to sit, be lit
by banks of candles where he simmers
in the poorly ventilated room
of a yet-to-be-anonymous artist.

Oh, but it must have been eye-watering
within those walls, rose-water or not.
And were the young man to release
Tamar's wrist for that oft-wished step

from flat dimensions to our world,
we would invite him but once
to parties where our own scents stay hidden,
buried under slathers of product.
And when he left (or even before)
we would likely make impolite asides,
a show of throwing open sashes for air
before lighting pitifully thin incense sticks—
like Absalom's deathly revenge on Amnon,
not so much too little as too late.

Picture Postcard from Long Beach, 1933

*These Southern California oil fields have wells drilled
so close together they resemble a deep forest.*
—caption

The card has been stuck behind attic junk,
my aunt's scraggly hand wishing all were here,
but no comment on the picture that today
brings a smirk from its quaint pride
(comparing man's oil wells to God's trees),
the photo hand-tinted, Monet-blurred
derricks sucking hydro-carbons beneath
ribboned blazes of an enhanced sunset.
But why expect eco-guilt from Aunt Dora?
She was blessed to live when humankind,
drunk on creation, reveled in its deeds,
seeing them all as good the way Yahweh did
after each of those arduous first days.
And perhaps they are. Maybe we *can* do no wrong—
strip-mining good, plutonium good,
space junk just more heavenly bodies
to track from backpacks on chill desert nights,
all adjuncts of *us*, most favored species,
this postcard proof we once revered ourselves
with the love that passeth all understanding,
which, of course, is mental health, isn't it?
Oh, but they must have been raw-glory days,
when the sacrifice of Long Beach's dunes
or those great swirls of carrier pigeons
was just the price of doing business,
our promised dominion over all that crawls,
walks, flies or slithers acknowledged,
endorsed, cashed in, spent willy-nilly.
We had to be about our Father's work.

Origins of Hell

When the Young Widow took her purse
and stepped quickly to the door,
we never dreamed she would be gone
forever as our Sunday School teacher.
We were Junior High IIs, in love
with her basically, which was why
we made arm-farts and called Jesus
"The Beatnik"—just trying
to get her grown-girl attention, that's all,
what was so different from her Bible self.
But we went too far.

The next Sunday Mr. Manning was there,
his face a capillary road-map
spanning quite the bumpy nose.
Easy to see now he had a drinking problem,
but at the time he was just old,
too old we felt sure, to take us on.

He leaned on his desk and passed around
a much-folded picture of Ginger
that smelled of his leather wallet.
Ginger was his old retriever
who had died on a hunt years ago,
barely making it back to shallow water.
"Retrieving herself," Mr. Manning said.
"Last thing old Ginger ever did."

After a shoe-scraping silence
we all started in on our own
dead-dog or lost-dog story,

Mr. Manning showing interest in each one,
yet he kept bringing it back to Ginger,
his sneaky lesson—
how retrieving yourself was getting saved,
how dog love, so unqualified,
equaled Faith, and how Sunday School
was our shot against rabies, the Devil.
The next week we were eager for more
news of Ginger, but instead Mr. Manning
went into a detailed account concerning
The Old Man in the Clouds
who kept the Big Book
that held a separate page
for every soul ever born.
Mr. Manning said that one day
we were all going to have to stand there
and be quiet while the Old Man
added up your life's score.

The following Sunday we discussed
the Fires of Hell, not so much
concerning their actual heat
but more how eternal they were.
Mr. Manning made the Fires interesting
by telling us of Saint Augustine
who pretty much invented Hell as we know it.
Yet at the same time, whether
it was the pain or the unendingness,
the Fires scared us because Hell
now seemed so closely bound with what
the Old Man saw on your Big Book page.
We all saw the Young Widow on ours.
We knew we had wasted our one

chance to ever be with her.
We grieved for sweet, brave Ginger.
We did not want to go to Hell.

Saint Augustine had Hell
set up so those in Heaven,
the ones with a good page,
had a clear view down to where
the rest of us were writhing
around like the poor ants
we sometimes fried with a
magnifying glass in the driveway.
This seemed poor sportsmanship,
gloating or something; it did not
fit in with the image of a kindly Saint
(well, he did have a few girlfriends),
living out his last years
on the north coast of Africa
before passing away peacefully just as,
far out in the Mediterranean,
the Vandals, having picked Rome clean,
were rowing south, singing
Vandal songs with very bad breath,
leaning into their oars, the whiff of land
and a fresh city closer, very close now.

When You Wait Too Late to Go to LA

for Gary Rhine

Hopi women still stretch to his *Rez-Robics*.
    All his native peoples' films, in fact, live,
but Rhino is dead, fallen from the sky,
    and you're here too late, too late to riff
commune sitcom pitches, pilot plots
    born of that upside-down world where you both
grew to men while inspecting each other
    for any semblance of bad-boy ego
those nights you waited outside tent birthings,
    midwife butlers in a homemade ambulance.
So you're too late, yes, but a day early
    for the wake and alone, left to question grief—
can it ever not be about yourself—
    before you opt for a Rhino-style goof,
a cruise down Santa Monica Boulevard,
    which your guidebook says used to be two lanes
snaking through orange groves, a scene long since
    gone to concrete strip-mall treadmill,
the last miles of a so tired Route 66
    dead-ending into the cold Pacific
where American dreams must re-invent
    or buy a very expensive wet-suit,
dreams tied to the Boulevard's call—*Head Shots!*—
    your cue to tap the brakes on the rental
for we could all use a better one, couldn't we?
    And why wait, for on corner after corner
the woo of *Head Shots!* wakes a seductive
    yet neurotic pull to dump the old shot
that's now terribly passé, so last block,

the slight sideways smile, what were you thinking?
And look, just past the Brentwood turn-off,
    here's a parking place under *Head Shots*!
a hint from some on-duty deity
    to stop, to try and rehab sagged cheekbones
(Rhino would have loved the cheesiness),
    the perfectly moussed dude and oh-so-built
dudette rising from their leather sofa
    in a synched display of ennui,
their perfect faces now marred by small frowns
    from the perhaps insurmountable
problems associated with your head
    that must hail from an antique land,
from past the valley even. But they're skilled,
    first slathering on pungent tan-gel
before blinding you with the concave discs
    while the woman in a Mylar sari
snaps off five shots (exhaling, "Yes!" for one),
    swipes your card, uploads your proofs and sends you
back out on the Boulevard where there's but
    a few blocks remaining for *Westward Ho!*,
the known world running out, almost done,
    your manifest destiny now to regret
all those Head Shots Past, the losers
    you stuck with too long, worst foot forward.
And combined with the Humboldt current's
    February chill plus the loss of Rhino,
it all conspires into a bad spiral
    for your seriously under-dressed self
because you're going to finish the continent
    on foot, the South, all else at your back now,
LA too much for the boy, LA where
    there's no more midnight trains anywhere—

there's just this eucalyptus grove and then
    the Pacific Coast Highway footbridge
leading to the Santa Monica Pier
    with its grumpy, get-off-my-lawn signage:

> *No skate-boarding.*
> *No roller-blading.*
> *Absolutely no overhead casting!*

all so opposed to Jim Morrison's
    long-ago promise, the one you trusted:

> *The West is the Best . . .*
> *The West is the Best . . .*
> *Get Here. We'll do the rest.*

advice you now clearly recognize
    as the babblings of an acid head for
you have got yourself here, and what of it?
    A chill wind, a dead friend, too many rules.
And even offshore, far out on the pier,
    it can't be, but it is . . . one last *Head Shots* chance,
this one less than confidence-inspiring,
    its sign leaning atop a ramshackle place,
no, it's a stand . . . reminiscent of what,
    there were others like this, where were they—
wait, yes, US 41 outside Tifton,
    a stretch of highway with competing signs
like worn-thin decimals born to repeat
    Boiled Peanuts!—those were the same words
every few miles, each shack somehow worse off
    than the last, each sign done up with spray paint
dripping down used plywood propped way too near
    open fires under steaming caldrons—

Boiled Peanuts same as *Head Shots* a shell game
 feeding on doubt, the promise of new.
But mostly there was joy from escaping
 the scratchy backseat once Daddy pulled over,
announced this was it, the one true stand,
 for he had spied red twine bags, Number Ones,
the too-wrinkled lady dipping deep,
 her ladle hauling them up, lost treasure,
hot briny goobers in a paper bag,
 what taste so much like the earth,
what taste so much like the ocean.

Toast

At the Galway hotel breakfast bar
I can't stop staring at the stack of toast
(think Inca temple) this guy is building,
what makes him snap, *An Irishman needs his toast!*
something I've been noticing actually,
how Ireland exalts toast, how it's a link
to some peat-fired genetic memory—
the stooped mother in black over a hot stove
preparing that ace weapon in their everyday
war against dampness—*Toast!*—the word itself
warm, a call to celebrate with a speech,
drinks held high to one's jolly good fellows.
It's Ed Sullivan's *Toast of the Town*
where I first saw the Beatles,
it's an aging cornerback beaten again.
It's what you're warm as.
It's the tip of your tongue making love
with the roof of your mouth each time
you say it, and it doesn't matter
if we're Irish or not, we come into
this world as wheat berries, we go out
as crumbs, and our life in the middle,
that's the jam—*Toast!*—the first three letters
an anagram for *Tao,* in Lao Tzu's words:

> *The harmony of one's personal will
> lining up with the justice of nature.*

And upon my return to the states
I'm wild to join in this toast business,
to buy a toaster, a big-box cheapo

for working-stiff proletariat toast.
But after plugging it in, I find out
the thing emits an unblinking blue light,
the annoying beam of product overkill.
Even when I don't want toast or I'm
even thinking of toast, there's that light
in the kitchen like a corner-boy going,
"Yo, I got your toast right here,"
its blue so the hue of police lights.
There is no subtlety to this light
like there was with the faint green light
at the end of the dock in *The Great Gatsby,*
a glow that is argued about to this day—
was the glow for his love of money?
Was it the light that Daisy emitted?
But the blue light just stares. It holds no *Tao,*
no stooped mother, no justice of nature.
The diode eye is so the opposite of toast
something has to be done—that's why Kathy
finds me on the floor with the toaster one night.
I have a hammer and a nail set.
I am Ulysses intent on justice,
and that one staring eye is you-know-who.
The blue light's a blight on the nobility
of the Irish, warmth, Lao Tzu, Gatsby.
In the name of all that's toast it must go.

On the Approach of Jehovah's Witnesses

There is a cadence to this walk of the sent
on Saturday morning, the plod of mules who
step steady, no-mind in everyday furrows.

So would that make us the pigweed or the crop?
Either way we hide, as put off by the men's
leather briefcases as the women's plumed hats,

a bit frivolous or perhaps even cocksure
for those bearing End-Time tidings of rapturous
Hell-fire, our coming fate as per Revelation,

a book one can't quite dismiss while crouched
behind curtains, sore afraid of what's outside—
the wrong end of a busybody, spiritual trumpet.

But for now they're across the street so we peek
as they climb the Jordans' steep steps flanked
by Tibetan prayer flags tattered in affirmation.

They knock and wait proselytizing minutes,
never suspecting we've already called the Jordans
before it's back down the steps and straight up

the next walk where shirtless renters greet
them with what look to be obscenities while
slamming the door so hard in the woman's face

she staggers to avoid a fall, one of her fuchsia
feathers drifting to the porch floor, wounded.
The men each take an elbow, a tableau of martyred

concern until she nods, and they're moving on,
no question, because there is another house, some
sustenance drawn in the process, surely not

from conversions but more from the uneven steps
and rude slams on this tape-loop of streets
with walls shielding trapped souls entreating,
Please, if it be Thy will, may we be spared.

You Probably Had to Be There

—after Kinnell's *The Apple Tree*

My Cambridge walking-tour stories fall flat
because I lack our guide's posh accent,
her vowels so trilling, so rounded
you want to have upper-class sex with them,
enunciation as a force of persuasion . . .
especially for hopeless Americans
whose push-pull with the koan of nobility
mirrors the plight of UFO nerds at night—
they yearn for the ship yet fear the probe.

It's the Newton legend that really flops,
how the gnarled apple tree by the old gate
descends directly, seed-to-tree-to-seed-to-tree
from the one that . . . well, you know . . .
For friends to accept this from my flat voice
would be to deny what we so treasure—
skepticism, the only thing holding us back
each time a Carnie yells, "Step right up!"

So no sale on the tree even though its apples
have obeyed a now-out-of-fashion law
(okay, light bends, but things still fall!).
They lie bruised, rotting, on their way to wine,
feeding Kinnell's worms who emerge, behold:

> *creation unopposed,*
> *the world made entirely of lovers . . .*

Now there's the target audience for yarns—

the smitten who stroll, bike, punt on the Cam.
Even when fed stretchers, obvious whoppers,
the lovers guild has standards, by-laws.
Their duty is to nod, to question not.

A Long Term Study on the
Effects of Intercessory Prayer

Funded by a big-name medical school,
here was a best-shot attempt
to resolve an abiding mystery,
complete with practiced petitioners
both vested and lay, all supplied
patient histories and diagnoses
(even photos for the visualizers),
with all prayers synchronized
for maximum healing firepower.
In fact, every aspect was handled just
as it would be were this a trial
for any new drug or procedure,
the only way findings could ever
be published in a major journal,
which meant there was a Control Group—
not so bad for the controlees
if they were denied fen-phen
or the hair-growth hormone that makes
erections resemble overcooked pasta.

But no. Here was an unapologetic
double-blind denial of prayer
for an unfortunate segment of humanity
on some teaching hospital's saddest floor,
rooms where green-fleshed televisions
radiated over cut-rate bouquets,
rooms where, in the name of a rude grant,
all clinical attentions were allowed
save the oldest one owning a name.
Yet as the study took pains to admit,

certain aspects were beyond their control
for inevitably word reached a niece
once removed in Barstow who, after reading
Aunt Mat's newsy Christmas card,
sighed at the mention of an ill cousin,
and, never realizing the harm
she was about to inflict on medical research,
kin found a quiet place. She prayed.

Fourth and Fifth Periods, 1962

Just before lunch Miss Martha Lynch did her best
to convey the shining promise of "new math" wherein
only 1's and 0's could be used for any computation.
She had just attended binary summer camp
and was feverish from her conversion.
"Computers can't understand the concept of 2,"
Miss Lynch explained in her dry-mouth drone
(people didn't hydrate very well back then).
"They can only read a 1 or a 0.
The switch is either on or off. Black or white."

It was our low blood-sugar hour,
and we thought her not only dull but deluded
to preach that 1's and 0's would change the world.
We weren't dumb. We knew about computers.
We had seen the massive Univac on TV,
Dave Garroway half-laughing at the thing
having to be packed in dry ice so as
not to overheat while doing whatever it did.
Here, at last, was common-ground with great aunts
appalled at the folly of modernity.

After lunch we ran to the sub-basement—
Print Shop!—where Mr. Falcon, in full leather apron,
taught us the intricacies, the deft touch
of setting moveable type upside down, backward,
each inky letter, each space, set just so before
it began, the thrilling violence that could easily
take a finger, a hand, even an arm,
what first smudged then smacked out perfect sheets
into the hopper, a process barely changed
from Whitman's—no, Swift's—no, Gutenberg's time.

Here was true communication that was
so removed from the impotent 1's and 0's Miss Lynch
kept insisting would become some class of code,
love letters to motherboards not yet conceived,
a baseless promise we rejected in favor of noise,
danger, Mr. Falcon's stink, legible copy!
Here was the information age come to fruition.
Here was the worldwide conversation in our hands,
and in celebration we sometimes smeared our faces—
tribal joy from this ink, key to kingdoms.

From Milton to Blake

This London walk from grave to grave
(planned online with red wine months ago)
has become, in the execution phase, a lens
through which the other's failings are noted—
what starts with map-snatches (first him then her)
while searching for St. Giles Cripplegate,
the medieval church so maddeningly close,
visible even, yet somehow protected (like her),
encapsulated (like him) by a modern
mixed-use development (them)
whose security codes repel all access
until workmen on tea-break point the way,
the one way, to Milton under his nave slab
where pipe organ lessons run scales. Check.

Satisfied, they continue down side streets,
their mapped-out shortcut to Blake that instead
erupts lunchtime workers on missions,
the two of them suddenly in-the-way,
buffeted, each now in bad-breakfast crisis,
her need to pee (McDonald's the one choice)
pushing him into a "Please! Not there!" sulk . . .
pushing her into a "You deny me this?" anger . . .
news agent boards screaming, *Shares Plummet!!*,
the poorest of omens lining the way
to Bunhill Fields where Blake's aboveground bones
are surrounded by even more crisp suits
taking lunch on iron benches, all in cell phone
dramas, all voices merging to one song,
and look, here's Defoe who must still bask
in his genius plot twist—footprints on the beach.

The Morning After
George Segal Died—6/10/00

They sit in the Princeton Burger king,
four elderly men, at least two Italian,
a window-table breakfast club
chewing first on the Yanks—they lost,
then Sammy's gut—it's winning,
before the one with the *Times* says,
"Least that damned artist died."
"What?"
"You know," he nods across Nassau.
"The one who did that damn sculpture."
Their heads all turn to the campus, precise.

The figures are life-size, bronze
weathered to an ebony: Abraham,
knife drawn . . . Isaac kneeling, bound.
The rope is quite remarkable.
All up against a neo-gothic chapel
undergoing buttress maintenance—
sand-blasts, tuck points, joint seals
behind a Construction Zone fence
that now chain-links next to Abraham's elbow,
poised at the words, Yahweh's pardon,
that first ever call from the Governor.

Danger. Hard Hat Area.

Two 55-gallon drums, some scrap lumber
and a Porta Potty stand in as Sinai scrub.
Genesis 22, the libretto, is fixed

to the chapel's granite near a plaque,
simple words regarding Kent State,
what had pissed-off the Burger King table,
what had earned a coffee damnation, casual
yet bitter, the ancient one-way ticket.
Inside the fence a hard-hatted
young man climbs from the scaffold.
Barely mid-morning, he's already soaked,
last night's liquors evaporating,
fruity even at this distance.
He raises a plastic gallon
water jug and drinks by Abraham,
his Adam's apple working, working.
He cares not for the sculpture,
its connection to an open-sore war
or likely even the buttresses, his work.
The Yanks, yes, he must care for them,
and tonight within some Jersey walls
he might well be the one tested,
the father who can choose to use
a knife or even his hands however,
the father who can listen or not.
And if his faith is pulled tight
beyond that every morning call,
beyond certain tolerances,
and if his unborn son turns one day
in some inevitably wrong way,
we will never find it written,
those particular begats because
lives these days are spared,
spared the curse of Intervention.

Checkpoint, Burkina Faso

Because he's holding your passport now,
this teen Gendarme with red beret and AK,
you know not to reach, to even want it back.
Better to fake a bored stare out the bush taxi
windows where women are lifting bananas
and plastic bags of water drooping like
engorged teats in tropical colors—
the waters thrust so close you can almost
see amoebas doing the backstroke.
Ramadan will be over tomorrow,
the women's eyes plead.
Surely you will buy? You will feast?

American hip-hop cranks from blown speakers,
The Ten Commandments of Crack:
    I been in this game so long, it made me
    an animal. There's rules to this shit.
    I wrote me a manual . . .
soundtrack for the boy-soldier's attentions
to each passport page, each stamp
in your thin blue book about an eagle.
Tribal scarifications, cat whiskers
at his eyes, announce that he was once
initiated into nighttime manhood,
an animist cosmos now jilted
for the assault rifle, the paycheck,
beret and boots—yes, these blackest boots
quite possibly swung the deal.

Outside, two boys are rattle-dancing
a tired foosball table, its homemade men
snipped from tin spin-swatting a taped-up ball
next to a mud mosque napping between prayers.
And just as you ask, why here?
Why this stretch of road *en brousse*
almost to the Mali frontier,
you notice the tree, one gray acacia,
shade for a paper and stamp table where
unsmiling officers in knock-off Ray Bans
extort from your fellow passengers.
And this is when gun metal comes cold
on your arm, the boy leaning low,
looking both ways, privacy a must
before he whispers, "Tupac?
Tu connais . . . Tupac Shakur?"

Prideful Buddhist

You leave college your senior year, become
a townie garbage-man in spiritual crisis,
the polite term for taking too much acid
too soon after reading *Franny and Zooey*
wherein Franny leaves her dreadful weekend date
to commence a new life of ceaseless prayer
right there in the restaurant bathroom—
her break the model for your break from . . . *all* . . . *this*.
Okay, you're inarticulate, but at least
you're not three chapters behind in everything
anymore, plus you're making a buck-fifty
an hour hanging on a bad-mufflered truck,
hopping off while the thing's still rolling
for the can-drag, the quick dump, the toss back
before a sharp whistle (which still needs work)
to Slim the driver, your parents in shock,
repeating, "This is just a phase, a phase . . . "
which, of course, is *their* constant mumbling prayer,
their concerns so the same as Franny's mom's
when she put the praying girl on their East Side couch,
brought in soup and smart brothers who only
made things worse rattling on about Noble Truths,
Bodhisattvas, all no help to her or you.
But at least you've stopped hiding from the war
you watch the poor fight on TV each night.
You will take a physical but until then
you make cowboy coffee in the morning,
and on cold nights you buy a short bag of coal
from Preacher's little shack by the side-tracks,
and when they switch you to *Leaves and Limbs*

you make a scene, a grand show of refusal
because it's an all-white crew, the cleaner truck
ruining everything, all your selfless aspirations!
But wait, now you've become Franny's bad date,
his Flaubert-paper-pride no different from yours
when any true seeker should know by now:
all trucks end up at the same dump.

Draughts of the Warm South

In My Grandfather's Ruined Cabin

The great-aunts shuffle through the rubble,
black pocketbooks held close, at the ready,

> *They took the dining room table. Laws . . .*
> *They broke every window, Lord, have mercy . . .*
> *They tore out the walnut shelves!*

I am six, confused—Who are . . . *They*?
The outhouse is horrifying enough
for a child half-reared by these women,
Edwardian hold-outs, my grandmother
the one sister to marry, endure sex,
go to France with her med student husband,
who, after studying with Madam Curie,
zapped so many tumors in the New South
he was able to buy this mountain acre,
these rooms that must have once been not broken.

But "Pop" is dead now, *gone on*, they say,
his beloved place on its own slow slide,
his wife and her sisters helpless, appalled
(an increasingly favorite word),
from confronting the low-side of life.
They'd been raised in Knoxville those summer nights
James Agee preserved for all time.
Their world had been all manners, honor.
Reading headlines from unbought newspapers
was, I was taught, the same as stealing.
And now senseless meanness, their best family
rooms trashed, debauched by Rabun county folk,
models for the locals Dickey would draft
to police the wild river (down two hills)

from the likes of us, Atlanta people,
a family fresh out of sober men
(my father will sell all this for bar debts).
I am the last great hope, only too late,
little more than a dress-up doll for them.
The world is changing. My aunts soon will die
the way we all do when days first go strange
then beyond redemption. Closing time.
The century's half spent, so much is too late.
Atoms have been split, radiation spilt
beyond all recall, loosed even here
into innocent June bugs and dust motes
caught in this haze over Warwoman Dell.

Cotton States Crossing

Burning the world to live in it is wrong.
—Wendell Berry

Life in a small southern railroad town
   means the quick trip across the tracks for beer
can evolve into a meditation
   on a slow-moving line of brimmed coal cars
hitting—*che-chung! che-chung!*—that one loose tie,
   club music rhythm in a too-bright club,
and next to your truck there's company,
   a Vietnamese woman weighed down,
twenty-five pounds of rice in each hand
   (the bags come with handles), her shoulder bones
starting to protrude through her skin-tight skin
   from the strain of keeping food off wet ground,
you both settling in, knowing this crossing
   starts that long uphill grade to Stone Mountain,
the train slowing now, the *che-chungs* dropping
   a note, high squeals kicking in, the soundtrack
to your private rolling graffiti show,
   the best from the Anthracite corridor,
and after *Philly Mo!* passes three times
   (brilliant leaning letters on grey hopper cars),
you roll down the window—*Excuse me, Ma'am,*
   you can set your rice in here while we wait.
But this is wrong. A breach. All about you.
   It forces her to now make an effort
(on top of all her other efforts)
   to avoid eye-contact with do-gooders.
Okay. Fine. You'll just lean back, curate
   these nuanced spray-can expressions of self,
the paint cost, the ladders, the heat from bulls,

all so Philly Mo could decorate cars,
live just like the *so long as men can breathe* thing.
    Philly Mo! and long-compressed carbon
taking a slow ride to some smoke stacked plant
    where the House-that-Jack-Built thing begins—
    This is the coal we burn to boil water
    that turns into steam that can turbine
    electrons to alternating frenzies,
    inchoate current for all God's children.

And up the stacks go those parts per million,
    you and the rice-holding woman watching
the same movie we've seen before,
    the one where we get all dystopic
just to keep our beer cold, or sure, boil rice,
    your beer going warm, her rice still heavy,
Philly Mo! still out there in switching yards,
    or maybe he's in Vo-tech . . . maybe jail.
Che-chung, Che-chung—and who will fix this tie
    under rails brave boys once killed for, died for?
And how much longer can a frail woman
    keep fifty pounds just inches off the ground?
And atop each coal car the cruelest joke—
    a solar panel! Properly aligned,
some CSX ad man's PR brainstorm,
    tropism panels tracking the same sun
that pressure cooked peat into the black rocks
    now ambling past at the mournful pace
funeral trains maintain. But today's last car
    does not hold a president in repose,
and the whole town has not shut down, turned out.
    Men are not holding their hats over hearts.
Little boys don't stand at attention, salute.

West African Church Picnic, Clarkston, Georgia

I pour the stuff to start sons and daughters fit for these States . . .
—Walt Whitman, *A Woman Waits for Me*

We're drawn to their pavilion by the PA
distorting letters then numbers, *N . . . 33, N . . . 33 . . .*
to tables of batiked, head-scarfed women
studying square cards—and here's what holds us:
we want to hear one of them yell, *Bingo!*
But the arrival of a young woman distracts,
baby in back-sling, gallon jug riding her head,
she moves with some regal understanding.
Late sunlight slants through the plastic jug
highlighting its unearthly lime-punch green,
what's close to the color of anti-freeze
or water cooling spent nuclear rods.
Women friends gather, exchange salutations
with her, with the baby, the wrong-color drink
still comfy until it is noticed, lowered
with grace, with smiles all around
for it's what she has brought to the picnic.
It is what she has carried the half-mile
from Thriftown, across the CSX tracks,
eight pounds fused atop her spinal column
the way she carried water as a girl
before boy soldiers came to her village.
Paper cups are produced, the stuff carefully poured,
not Whitman's patriotic semen, no,
this is a different class of wet, so bad
we want to yell, Stop! Don't drink that stuff!

But they do . . . they do . . . they partake
as though it were their duty for it is their duty . . .
to take the worst this country has to offer
and transform it into life force, breast milk even.
It's a pine tree transubstantiation—
corn syrup, dyes, and benzo-sulfates
consecrated to a toast by pure trust.
They smile. The baby is fit for these States.

Atop the Great Temple Mound

Far below us winds the Etowah River
where Pumpkinvine Creek empties, defining
the Mound Builders' ceremonial plaza,
what Pa Tumlin no doubt called *bottomland,*
its deposits of silt layering yearly
until the family's yields must have been
the envy of all Bartow county.
The Interpretive Center informs us that
generations of Tumlins worked the plaza,
first from behind mules, traces draped
across hard antebellum necks before
Sherman, Victoriana, the Great War
came and went, leaving Tumlin men
to ride their one cylinder John Deere,
pop-popping Depression years away
when they must have trapped river trout
same as the Mississippians, whoever they were.

What must that farming family have made
of this half-acre risen five stories tall
smack in the middle of their best field?
They had to have climbed the ancient stone steps
(now buried for safekeeping) to picnic,
court, or simply gawk as we do today.
And surely the men folk calculated
the toil, appreciated how many years,
how many baskets of dirt, ruined backs,
tampings, wash-outs, slides, do-overs
every bit of it now a monument
to them, the new kings who payed taxes
on what had been abandoned by those
who some say rode west on Spanish ponies

to a buffalo cosmos, limitless
between great plains and a bowled sky
what's so removed from our vista today—
signage *absolutely* prohibiting
"any religious activity or ceremony" . . .
leaving us to revel internally,
take in the river, the lesser mounds, and
yes, the Bow and Arrow Trailer Court
hard up against the state park fence,
doublewides splayed like fat dominoes,
the game just getting under way.

Where Flesh Begins

The old man with two boys in a Carolina skiff
    asks permission to fish here even though
everybody in these parts knows the salt-marsh
    creeks are tidal, free as the world's ocean,
but it's the dock where we sit sipping coffee,
    that's what they're after, the pilings actually,
barnacled habitat of sheepshead, the tasty
    prehistoric-looking fish that they proceed
to yank, yank, yank from the low-tide murk
    as if this were some Kiwanis pool at a fair—
all done with cane poles, tiny crabs as bait
    and a wrist flick quick as a frog's tongue.

We try not to stare, admit that we're guests
    here ourselves because it's intoxicating
how they think we own this Cumberland dock;
    it's what one shoots for when traveling,
to be taken as a local, to get inside a place,
    but either the old man really knows
we're from the city, which is probable,
    or else he's just feeling expansive
from hauling up so many sheepshead,
    for he answers the question we so want to ask.
"It's the feel," he says. "That's all there is
    to it. You jerk right before they bite."

We nod, "yup," as if we knew that already
    which is a bad move because then he shuts up
like maybe he thinks he's boring us
    instead of making us crazy with desire to ask,

"Wait, what does it feel like right before they bite?"
    And so we miss a sweet chance at passed-down
knowledge of the physical world because
    we're pretending to be who we're not
same as we would have if a Parisian on the Metro
    had given us a world-weary shrug at loud
Americans braying about the lack of orange juice—
    we'd shrug back, accept an offered world.

Before long they've run themselves out of bait
    so the old man grounds the skiff on the mudflats
that the new-moon tide has now fully exposed,
    and there go both boys, climbing out onto, into
the sucking, fetid blackness where they crouch,
    arms cocked, still as site sculptures
yet sinking as slowly, slowly hundreds
    of thumb-nail crabs venture from hundreds
of holes, the fatal choreography of hunger
    overcoming caution, and here it is:
what we'd just read about in *The Sea Around Us,*
    Rachel Carson saying, here, right here!

is first flesh created by the salt marsh,
    crab soma constructed from the whole cloth
of algae, plankton, seawater, sunshine
    and salts only to be snatched by giggling boys.
We consider offering them this knowledge as perhaps
    a trade for the secret of when to jerk,
but it's not a fair trade—ours is from a book,
    while his was handed down from a long line of daddies.
Instead we watch them hook exo-skeletons just so
    (another trick), before lowering the crabs,

an offering to the many-toothed sheepshead
    who are helpless to not nibble, get jerked,
measured and layed out in a cooler,
    freezer-food for the crown of creation.
We compliment their catch and ask where
    they're from. "Irwin County," he says. "A ways."
"Ahhh, Irwin County," we go. "Wasn't that
    where they finally captured Jefferson Davis?
He was hiding and wearing a dress. Isn't that the story?"
    The old man frowns and gives his pole a snatch,
"Lies," he says. "Those are Yankee lies."

First Commune Winter

Before we knew this would be serious
we skipped stones down the creek,
grasshopper games, death to water striders.
We sketched plans for unroofable domes
while neighbors chopped, stacked oak splits.

Days shortened yet macro and micro still spoke,
giardia burps a potent birth control,
the Mennonites' old mare (thrown in on a trade)
came up lame, her hooves so packed with thrush
the chipped-out stench brought crows thinking, *carrion!*

Canning jars didn't seal, and out on Highway 20
semis disturbed the peace with their jake brakes.
Wood smoke hung, molecules too cold to escape
scrub-oak hollows, folds in a mapped blanket
the county taxed and sometimes repossessed.

We sat za-zen, chanted *Ommmm*, and made sure
the Primitive Baptists knew about it.
Kerosene leaked on brown rice we ate anyway—
Take that, pinworms! Frozen tire ruts twisted ankles.
Fence post vultures spread wings to a brief sun.

The miller refused our Deaf Smith wheat—too hard
for his stones, he said, so we boiled wheat berries
which never once got done. Sorghum sweetened
cereal gave babies the shits. Wet oak sizzled,
put fires out; piss jars clouded the second day.

Hunger almost hurt. Distant parents, off-the-clock,
accepted charges in the curbed street world
we left for campus quads then blighted fields,
peyote tea on solstice morning, tape-handled ax lost
beneath snow, entropy loose, uncaring.

Our Liberian Street Preacher, Miss Edna, Makes Her Rounds at Six in the Morning

Actually she screams more than preaches—
    You must Pray! Pray! Pray!
words that destroy all hope of more sleep,
become part of your first-blink check-list
for the coming day . . . pray . . . yes. I must pray . . .
And now she has set off the neighborhood dogs,
fox hounds who will never see a fox,
who instead bay at this too-loud woman
shaking her black book on the reggae beat,
the one and the three, not the two and four,
what I find genetically impossible.
And this is how one wakes up in Clarkston—
pray, pray, bark, bark, pray, pray, Jesus, Jesus, woof, woof -
Miss Edna marching on into her day
where there is no alternative
but to spread the word just as Matthew 28,
that most activist of verses, said:
Go ye therefore and teach all nations.

But wait. Didn't I, a Methodist teen,
give the collection plate extra quarters
after the Congo mission slide show?
Yes, and here they are coming back at me,
slapping me upside my sleeping head,
for if you're serious about the Godless,
what better place to start than America
where *Temptation Island Wife Swap*
is bounced off satellites, a warning,

to the world: Don't end up like us!
Miss Edna a Christian Bodhisattva
living those vows: The lives of the unsaved
are innumerable. I vow to save them,
"them" being us between thread-count sheets,
upscale pillows wrapped around our heads.

Jody Leaves the County

Barefoot now, having come to the river,
he undresses, folding each garment
carefully on a bureau-height boulder,
the flannel shirt acrid, an eye-watering
reminder of what she must have been smelling—
his cornered and fermenting stink.

She said he should take a nice walk?
Fine. He would show her, walk a straight line
out the back door and keep right on going,
ducking the 3-strand barb-wire, past hay fields
before slowing to stuff his pockets with pecans
beneath diagonal rows of just-shook trees.

Now supplied, he presses on through stands
of blackberries and Queen Anne's lace just burnt
from a first frost yet defiant still, then further,
into a sumac brake, each step lower now,
leading to the mud-slick banks of Kelly Creek
rain-swollen and beckoning with intent.

There is really no question—he will follow,
let it lead him to this wide scope of motion,
brown creek water meeting up with slateish
greater water, the river, whose lazy width
accommodates a path of mammoth outcrops,
stepping stones for some yet-to-come giant.

On the far bank is a US Forest Service sign
proclaiming to humans, deer and beaver
the rules of legislated wilderness,

how you can come here and be welcomed,
but that no ATVs (same as gossip, he hopes)
will be allowed purchase. He eats some pecans

before fashioning a necklace of his sneakers,
pressing his folded clothes to his head
with one hand and wading in, the water
cold yet tonic, its bottom turning
quickly from gravel to muck to ooze,
his right foot leading, testing for holes.

Cold water at autumnal gonads just
doesn't seem right. He recoils then continues,
sneakers floating now, to the second rock
where he rolls up (throwing his dry clothes first)
on granite still holding the sun's earlier warmth.
He is mid-river, county line on all maps,

and all around him the flat current
seems in no hurry to go join the Altamaha,
help continue its imperceptible fall
across an old sea-floor to the world's grey ocean.
Looking downstream, shivering now, he sees
none of that, yet he knows it's all there.

Aunt Weeza Sees a Condom
on the Side of the Road

No warning, no sense of finality,
the Cutlass just quits, that's all,
and since she avoids all fast lanes
it's doable, even with this sudden
power-steering loss, to ease over,
the car quiet now yet moving still,
in a 19th century way, tires crunching
rocks as though pulled
by tiring, invisible horses.

She tries a few re-cranks
before it's button the cardigan
and step out into the windy degrees
where rude vehicles, some arrogant,
continue their amazing progress,
mocking baby steps,
her five-and-a-halves unsteady
on ground that at some point
must have been an equal in creation.
But like poor relations,
this pushed-down fescue
has been written off,
become a linear dump for McTrash,
unapologetic plastic, faded beer cans,
tire casing snake skins, spent.

She recalls a nearby Rebel Mart
and proceeds, humming tuneless hymns,
one hand fixed to her sweater's
top button as though the garment might
pull free at any moment, seduced

by a semi's mud-flapping call.
But it's the everyday threat of a broken hip,
that's what keeps her eyes disciplined,
scanning each ankle-turning step,
that's how she sees it
the way you see the dead jellyfish
instead of the sand dollar,
which is why she stops at the cloudy mass
because it is, after all, something.
And in that moment's pause,
the whoosh-whish nearby,
she is not so much disgusted
as struck by how used up it is—
noble completion, a collapsed
dried-together skin pushed out a window,
forgotten, its one little life over,
this one shot we all get.

Just One of the Ways We Stay Alive

I took him for a tired Mormon.
Kathy thought he was heat-addled,
perhaps lost in a diabetic wooze,
something surely *off* about the way
he wandered into our front yard as though
all this were his, which, in a way it was.
"I was born in this house," he hollered,
pointing to a front bedroom window.
And then we were inviting him in
where the twelve-foot ceilings were pronounced,
"Too short, not as tall as I remember."

Old Mrs. Malone, we found out, used to keep
chickens next door. Fifty cents.
"Mama'd put two quarters in my hand,
and say, 'Go get us supper.'"
He paused, his red face leaning into ours,
"But I killed them back here, in your driveway."
He sliced at his own neck perhaps hoping
to somehow shock us with the pull of death,
what prompted me to counter with my own story—
African boys in our Peace Corps daughter's
village slitting chicken necks just so,
what made them stagger, pump their bodies dry.
My story though was borderline hearsay,
it came out wrong, vaguely competitive.
But he didn't seem to notice, he showed
polite interest as if nothing could ruin
this birth-place fugue state, what was now

progressing to Viet Nam, how this house,
his mother, the quarters, old Mrs. Malone
had all prepared him for a jungle war,
his chicken-plucking worth to a Major.
"That's what kept me in the rear," he said.
"That's what kept me alive."

Funeral Fridge

It waits in the Fellowship Hall basement,
plugged in of course, on-duty
even before the belt-sagging men
arrive with the church hand-truck,
death's ripple having begat
a shared sense of grim-faced purpose,
the succession of chores known well—
first directions, then grunting, *Easy there!*
while humping it into the pick-up bed
and keeping the thing somewhat upright
during the ride to that house whose driveway
is inevitably packed, which will mean
backing up on the grass to the carport
before the slightest door knock, softest words,
No, no, don't bother them. Just say it's here.

And so it is. Ready for the overflow—
covered dishes, meat platters, pies,
the crass yet always-consumed box of chicken,
and casseroles, glory be to the casseroles
Tupperwared, Reynolds-wrapped,
arrayed in the old Maytag that now stands
where the dead used to jingle change
while worrying that the squirrels were back.
And in a week or so, after pine needles
have mounded in drifts against its side,
about the time the door seal has grown
sticky from sweet tea spillage,
the survivor now begins to worry
that the hard pulls, the exertion required
for door yanks will perhaps be *their* undoing . . .
And so the call is made: Come get it.

Communal Mule

—Tennessee, 1971

He came concealed in the womb of Mabel,
one of our Belgian mares, a lazy team
we had bought from the canny Amish
who, by law, never part with good horses.
And then one morning there he was, wobbly,
sapling legs barely supporting such ears,
all of us swiftly in love, the deal's sting
now long gone because we were laughing last,
waiting in line to pet him, Barnabus,
the name that so fit, snuff-dipping neighbors
toasting our fortune before, in short words,
advising that he would have to be "shaved"
to be of any use, to not hurt us.

We did not eat meat or even honey,
so to have a pet (what he was) castrated,
well, it just wasn't going to happen.
No, we would surround him with calming love
same as we "fixed up" mental patients
by first throwing away their meds for
we assumed love's power spanned all species
even though we did find ourselves chasing
relapsed bi-polar friends through briary woods,
even though Barnabus soon started in
with first bites, then frog-quick pole-axing kicks
that put his handlers on crutches for weeks.
Soon only the purest girls dared feed him,
but when he kicked one of them that was it.
He was given to a local logger,

and, after the procedure, a much-subdued
Barnabus was sometimes seen snaking logs
from hollows where skidders could not go,
mule sightings on wintery roads that made us
stop our truck, and, helpless to do otherwise,
we approached him like blind men, arms forward,
still wary until that first touch between eyes
that regarded us with a glazed calm,
his pungence cueing recall of gone times,
but our own stink—wood smoke, dope smoke, gear lube—
produced only cold-fog snorts, harness shakes.
He was changed. He didn't know who we were.

For Cherryl

*I am making a quilt whose working title is "Race," and I'd like you
to craft a piece of text on a single moment from your life in which
you understood what race in our/your world means*
—from *A Call for Artists*

Most days it's me and Carrie in the kitchen, and oh yeah, her stories
on the radio like *Search for Tomorrow* with that organ, me with my
men on the floor, her with the pressing, shaking water from an old
ketchup bottle with ice pick holes in the top, and Carrie's, "Mmm,
Mmmmmm, MMMM!" when the voices in her stories reached for
something, when the organ stabbed at a chord before the same
Ovaltine commercial we'd just heard ten minutes ago, before we
shared bloated hot dogs on Merita bread with Gebhardt's chili,
Carrie saving the cream off the top before she poured my glass of
milk. All of this normal. Utterly normal—me, her, the pressing, my
men, the stories, chili, steam, her car fare, two coins on the front
table, all normal except for a day when her car fare was missing
(someone forgot), the hour late, a decision made, Carrie easing into
the back seat of my aunt's Mercury, a last-second, best-effort
tantrum allowing me to come too, the strange turns off Boulevard,
my aunt announcing, "Buttermilk Bottoms," like she was a bus
driver, the long hill down, down, the sun left behind, down to
where the Civic Center now stands, down streets jammed with
double-porched houses like layer cakes at some distant point white-
washed, the houses so close to the now-dirt streets, all of it a scene,
each porch alive top and bottom, boys running in the street, wood
smoke hanging over all, hop-scotching girls, rocking-chaired
grannies, greens-from-a-truck, a scene, men on a corner waving our
passage, Carrie able to find something specific out of it all, pointing,
"Just up ahead. Past that tree," a little boy locking my eye as I
scoot up so the front seat can fold, so she can work to get out.
This is another world. This is where Carrie lives.

Faulkner, Jung and the 60 Cycle Hum

On a Monday night I'm sitting home reading Faulkner—
        a vague punishment the way some don't drink
on Mondays as a half-assed penance for getting so out-there
                over the weekend,
and there's this other, hovering part of me that's admiring
        myself for traversing these side-slopes of literature,
not that the Faulkner is boring because he's telling me
                this story of Joe Christmas,
            a Mississippi cracker whose secret is
        that he's half-black even though he passes for white,
but it's the Thirties so he's full of self-loathing
        tinged with the fear of discovery when terrible things
are sure to happen and do happen,
                                so yeah, it's a good yarn,
and the college radio station is going in the background
        because I have this vanity around staying *au courant*
with post-punk bands (although I would never
        say *au courant* to anyone with a piercing),
plus between songs you get to hear college undergrads
        with bad adenoids mangle words that anyone in college
should have at least mouthed by now,
                like calling the Cocteau Twins,
                the *Cock-a-two Twins*
meaning they have never even said the name, John Cocteau,
        so anyway as I'm feeling snugly and virtuous watching
myself read Faulkner, the undergrad deejay says,
        "Okay, that last song was by the Athens band,
Joe Christmas."

Which makes me sit up and go, Whoa!
            Synchronicity, what Jung said was never
    a coincidence, and maybe Jung should be my next
Monday punishment book, if, of course, I ever finish
    The Faulkner with its words, words, words
stretching across double pages with no paragraphs,
    dialogue, ellipses, gaps or anything but words,
and then I'm recalling what Jung said about neurosis,
    how it is the suffering of the soul
which has yet to find its true meaning.
And maybe this is my neurosis: to imagine
    I have to read important books as a class of punishment,
while my interior smarty-pants struggles to come up
    with an exception to Jung's definition, like, say,
Woody Allen whose neuroses *are* his soul's true
    meaning, that is, they keep him completely busy, sane—
but the undergrad deejay is interrupting me with,
    "Hey, I have two tickets to see the Swans this weekend
for the first caller who can tell me, who just read the
    Cliff Notes last semester, from what great novel
does the character, Joe Christmas, come from?"
    This makes me snap the book shut, turn to Kathy
and say, "I just won two tickets to go see the Swans."
    And she says, "That's nice, but find somebody else
to go with you,"
    and as I walk to the phone I'm thinking,
    hmmm, maybe Jon, this younger friend of ours
who looks like Sting and attracts women who think
    they deserve beauty which usually makes
for an interesting time,
    and I'm not rushing to the phone

because Synchronicity has spoken.
                                It is meant to be,
                                and it shall be served.
Plus there is not a chance anyone else will call in
with the answer because this is the station that for months
ran a promo with a fakey old man voice going,
                        "Call me Ahab, but when I'm not out
                                chasing white whales, I listen to 88.5"
    And I had even called in twice to complain that,
Doh! The first sentence of *Moby Dick* is,
"Call me Ishmael"!
        Both times though they acted like I was a whack-job
so when the undergrad deejay answers I just say,
                "Light in August."
And he screams like he had a bet with somebody
that no one
            would get it, but the next weekend there are my tickets
waiting at the box office, which is good because the show
        is sold out, Jon and I edging in with all the poseur punks
and the suburban punks and the wannabe Goths,
        the hall so dark all you can see are the little amp lights
up on stage, as slowly, subtly we begin to have
        an awareness of a noise,
                no, it's not a noise, it's a vibration,
what barely inhabits the realm of perception, a hum,
        not getting any louder, but you become more and more
aware of it the longer it keeps hummmming along
        because certain cranial bones, important ones,
are beginning to resonate with the hum,
        not that Jon is noticing because two really cute girls
                are already talking to him,

but behind them the pierced and the tattooed alike are putting
    their hands over their ears, and this guy next to us says,
        "Aww, Jesus, not the 60 cycle hum.
        I hope nobody in here is an epileptic."
And that's when I start to get irritated with the noise,
    me thinking: Well, I guess this is it. I'm way too old
for these shows. Who am I trying to kid?
    And the hum keeps humming along, not rising or falling
but morphing into a feedback loop like when you're
    tripping on acid, and you get palpitations from
that awareness of your own heart beating,
    its lub-dubbing simplicity a reminder
    of how precarious existence really is,
the bad dream of playing solitaire with mortality
    upon us all, and that's when this huge skinhead
gets up on a chair and screams,
        "Turn that fucking shit OFF!"
Which, as it turns out, is the signal for the Swans
    to come out, plug in and start playing,
them having this concept around their shows sort of like
    Andy Kauffman did where the idea is to first
try and piss off some of the people who have paid
    to come see you,
        and in this way a true dramatic tension
        will be achieved rather than
        the old-timey version
        which requires a suspension of disbelief,
what might be a deconstructivist assumption but
perhaps not,
    and the whole thing is beginning to remind me
of Faulkner,

how there was no gap in the 60-cycle hum
　　being a good bit like one of his paragraphs that go
on and on, the way you turn the page only to see two more
　　pages of words, words, words stretched out, limitless,
and if he hadn't gotten drunk as a coot and fallen
　　off that horse and killed himself, he'd likely still
be hammering out those pages, pages, pages,
　　but anyway, the Swans put on a good show,
　and when it's over Jon says he's leaving
　　with one of the girls or maybe both of them, who knows,
and I go home where Lucy, our grown daughter,
　　is staying up late talking with Kathy, telling her
about this old lady, almost a street person but not quite,
　　who had come up to their table that day
in the Piccadilly where Lucy was having lunch with Jasmine,
　　her ten-year-old daughter,

　　　　　　　　　　　and Lucy knew,

　　　　　　　　　　　she so knew

this lady was going to be trouble, and she was right because
　　the old lady stopped, pointed to Jasmine and asked
in a very loud voice as though she were hard of hearing,
　　"Is her father black?"
Which, looking at Jasmine is a very obvious question,
　　and Lucy said, "Yes,"
the next table starting to laugh a little by now,
　　but the old lady isn't through yet, she points again,
and in that same too-loud voice goes,
　　"You know, her grandchildren will be Octoroons."
And that gets several Piccadilly tables laughing,
　　But as Lucy is telling the story, it's like she sort of
thinks it's funny, God bless her,
but what it does to me though

is throw me right back into the synchronicity deal,
how Jung invented the word for one thing, but also it's
    how the old lady is straight out of *Light in August*,
what makes me want to repeat that Faulknerism,
    "The past is not dead; it's not even past,"
a line most associated with Spanish moss on live oaks
    when those words were actually spoken
in a Harvard dorm room, not that it matters because
    I decide not to tell Lucy the quote, for it would just be
my shadow, my sad attempt to still be instructive to a
    daughter already grown, you know, the suffering
of my soul looking for an outlet—so instead
    I just say I have a headache leftover from the Swans,
their 60 cycle hum, which is, after all, the truth, and so
    I say, good night; I go upstairs and go to bed.

About the Author

Rupert Fike's work has been published in *Rosebud, The Georgetown Review, storySouth, Borderlands, Texas Review of Poetry, The Cumberland Review, The Cortland Review, Natural Bridge* (University of Missouri at St Louis), *Atlanta Review, Snake Nation Review, Backwards City Review, FutureCycle, Dark Sky Magazine, A Celebration of Southern Poets* (Kennesaw University Press) and others. He has been nominated for a Pushcart prize in poetry (*Java Monkey Speaks*) and short fiction (*Rosebud*). A poem of his is inscribed in a downtown Atlanta plaza, and he has had several one act plays produced by the Alliance Theatre Interns for Theatre Emory. His non-fiction book, *Voices from the Farm*, edited accounts of life on this country's largest spiritual community, The Farm, is now available in paperback. *Lotus Buffet*, his first poetry collection, was a finalist in the Brick Road Poetry Contest 2010.

Rupert Fike reads his poems and conducts workshops at high schools and middle schools in the Atlanta area. He lives with his wife, Kathy, in Clarkston, Georgia not far from their daughters and grandchildren. Kathy and Rupert spent eight years on The Farm, a spiritual community in middle Tennessee which they helped found in 1971 after several years in the bay area. He is working on a book of poems based on The Farm experience.

POETRY PRESS

Our Mission

The mission of Brick Road Poetry Press is to publish and promote poetry that entertains, amuses, edifies, and surprises a wide audience of appreciative readers. We are not qualified to judge who deserves to be published, so we concentrate on publishing what we enjoy. Our preference is for poetry geared toward dramatizing the human experience in a language rich with sensory image and metaphor, recognizing that poetry can be, at one and the same time, both familiar as the perspiration of daily labor and outrageous as a carnival sideshow.

BRICK ROAD

POETRY PRESS

Also Available from Brick Road Poetry Press
www.brickroadpoetrypress.com

BRICK ROAD
POETRY PRESS

About the Prize

The Brick Road Poetry Prize, established in 2010, is awarded annually for the best book-length poetry manuscript. Entries are accepted August 1st through November 1st. The winner receives $1000 and publication. For details on our preferences and the complete submission guidelines, please visit our website at www.brickroadpoetrypress.com.

42979598R00071

Made in the USA
Charleston, SC
10 June 2015